The Concept of Evil

by Derek McMillan

Edited by Angela McMillan

An analysis of the concept and presentation of evil in Tolkien's novel "The Lord of the Rings"

Contents

1) Introduction

2) The power of darkness

3) The flame of Anor and the flame of Udun

4) The persuasive voice of evil

5) Oft evil will shall evil mar

6) The role of nature

7) Dark Satanic Mills

8) The Ring of Power

9) Conclusion

Introduction

This book examines the concept and presentation of evil in Tolkien's novel, "The Lord of the Rings". Although I have concentrated on the "Lord of the Rings", I have also made use of the Silmarillion which provides a 'background' and to some extent a dictionary which has aided my exploration of Middle Earth. In particular, the music of the Ainur proved a useful source of themes in the novel.

I have taken account of Tolkien's warning in his introduction to the novel -"As to any inner meaning or message, it has in the intention of the author none. It is neither allegorical nor topical ... I think that many confuse 'applicability' with 'allegory'; but the one resides in the freedom of the reader, and the other in the purposed domination of the author."

The Lord of the Rings was published at a time when great events such as the Second World War, the growing threat of the atom bomb and a "Dark Lord in the East" called not Sauron but Stalin, were fresh in the minds of its readers. In some ways I think it has a greater appeal to readers of that generation than it would have had for earlier generations. For example, I think that the terror of the flying Nazgul and the aerial bombardment of Minas Tirith would have had a. special meaning for those who had experienced the Blitz in London and the flying shadow of the VI. To say this is in no way to suggest that the novel is about Fascism or Stalinism, but where I feel that a particular application of Tolkien's ideas illuminates those ideas I have indicated the fact.

Evil performs an aesthetic function in the novel by providing a background of contrast against which the good characters shine more brightly. The machinations of Mordor put the good characters to the test, in particular bringing out the bravery of the least "heroic" figures - the hobbits. Tolkien has managed, by his combination of a Quest and a Crusade in the plot, to make good appear more attractive and interesting than evil. Whereas Milton's Satan is in the forefront in the first two books of Paradise Lost, Tolkien's Sauron is never actually seen but remains "remote and yet a present threat". He is a purely negative figure and his narrowed vision is emphasised. The novel is so designed that the reader never gets close enough to Sauron to sympathise with him.

In the novel, the negative, uncreative nature of evil (which I deal with more fully in Chapter I) is ultimately self-defeating., as can be seen from Illuvatar's words to Melkor - "And thou, Melkor, shalt see that no theme may be played that hath not its uttermost source in me, nor can any alter the music in my despite, for he that attempteth this shall prove but mine instrument in the devising of things more wonderful, which he himself hath not imagined." Thus, to use Theoden's aphorism "Oft evil will shall evil mar." (Chapter 4)

Although Tolkien's myth is not overtly Christian, I think that it can be shown to deal with the fundamental problem of evil in a Christian way. In Christian terms the problem is: how can evil exist among creatures created by, and in a world created by, a God who is wholly good? The aesthetic function of evil and its ultimately self-defeating nature are part of the answer, but they do not resolve the problem of the source of evil. St Augustine saw the origin of evil in Man's God-given free will: "For when the will abandons what is above itself, and turns to what is lower, it becomes evil - not because that is evil to which it turns but because the turning itself is wicked." (City of God XII 6) Thus Melkor, forgetting that his powers originated from Illuvatar , sought to create something which was entirely his own. Significantly the first things he created were "bitter cold immoderate" and "heats and fire without restraint" (Silmarillion p9) (see Chapter 2) which only served to enhance Illuvatar's original design.

Jung's theory of archetypes in the collective unconscious helps to clarify this issue. Jung saw "the old man" as an undifferentiated archetype - "beyond good and evil, the superior master and teacher, a pointer of the ways, the pre-existent meaning concealed in chaotic life which Western man tends to differentiate into "black and white magicians" (Integration of the Personality p86) This points to the importance of good and evil as man-made concepts (see Chapter 5) and casts light on the functions of Gandalf and Saruman.

Gandalf s adoption of Saruman's abandoned colour, his dramatic statement: "I am Saruman, Saruman as he should have been." (p5l6) and Gimli's "Like and yet unlike." (p60l) emphasise the similarity of the two. However, Saruman's pride has led him to turn from the path of true wisdom (see Chapters 3 and 6 for a fuller treatment of the consequences) In turning from a higher good to a lower, Saruman is ultimately brought very low indeed and is only capable of "a little mischief in a mean way." His refusal to leave the ruin of Isengard echoes Satan's idea that it is "better to rule in Hell than serve in Heaven" but Tolkien emphasises how squalid such a resolve really is.

We often refer to a desire to dominate others as a desire to "play God" but for Tolkien that is exactly what God does not do. Gandalf, who is a steward of the secret flame which is identified with Illuvatar in the Silmarillion, unlike Saruman or Sauron, rejects the domination of the wills of others which the ring would give him (see Chapter 7) (incidentally, it should be noted that desire for the Ring is fundamentally no less evil than actually using it - as the corruption of Boromir, Saruman and Denethor indicate)

The terms in which Tolkien sees the relationship between free will and determinism are clearly outlined in the Silmarillion where "the Valar perceived that the world had been but foreshadowed and foresung, and they must achieve it." (Silmarillion p20) Likewise Frodo, for example, was "meant to receive the Ring" but has to exercise his free will in renouncing it (why he does not finally do so is dealt with in Chapter 2) Gildor's unwillingness to give advice and Galadriel's warning about the visions in her mirror, Elrond's refusal to lay any burden on the Ringbearer, all emphasise the importance of personal choice.

I would not suggest that, Tolkien has actually achieved a resolution of the philosophical issue of free will and determinism (or divine providence in this instance). For example he does not explain why a creature created by divine goodness should turn from a higher good to a lower good. In fairness this was not his purpose and even those who have set themselves the task have never yet succeeded.

Mythology differs from legend in that it contains nothing which is "true" in the Gradgrind factual sense of the word. However, as I have attempted to show, Tolkien's myth contains a good deal of "truth" of another kind. For want of a better term I have tended to call this "poetic truth". (see Chapter 3)
In a sense these truths are not new but, on the contrary, eternal:

"Good and ill have not changed since yesteryear: nor are they one thing among elves and another among men. It is a man's part to discern them, as much in the Golden Wood as in his own house." (p459)

It is no accident that the last two chapters show the hobbit heroes rooting out the evil in the fields that they know. The transfer of the battle between good and evil from the romantic heights and depths of Gondor and Mordor to the "ordinary" world of the Shire brings home to the reader the idea that these high ideals of poetic truth (which are often expressed in simple aphorisms – see 'Conclusion') are relevant to everyday life.

It is significant that Tolkien rarely if ever draws any distinction between 'beautiful' and 'good' or 'evil' and 'ugly'. Although the distinction between appearance and reality is drawn in the presentation of Aragorn who 'looks foul and feels fair' (pl88) but is later transformed. Also Saruman undergoes a reverse transformation. However it is not a major theme. There is an almost symmetrical organisation of completely evil and completely good characters.

Compare, for example, the elves and the orcs. Elves have beautiful names, are fair to look upon, have a musical language, love living things such as trees and are slender and graceful. The orcs have names like 'Ugluk', ugly looks, a harsh guttural language, delight in destroying living things and are squat and bow-legged. The food of elves is delightful, that of the orcs would disgrace McDonald's! The attempts of Sauron (and later of Saruman) to produce a Master Race was the cause of these ghastly creatures and is a function of the inability of The Shadow to create. I will deal with this more fully in the next Chapter.

The power of darkness

Throughout the novel, Tolkien tends to use black as a symbol of vile. Thus, Mordor is "the Black Land" (passim), Sauron's hand as "black and yet burned like fire" (p270) Saruman is denounced as "a black traitor" (p494), Gollum is "the black sneak" (p960) and so forth. Undoubtedly this has certain racial connotations. All the good characters, such as the white rider Gandalf and the distinctly Aryan riders of Rohan are white Westerners. The evil ones are mainly black Southrons and swarthy Easterlings.

The theme of racial purity is touched on in the book. For example, Saruman the White becomes Saruman of many colours (p276) which partly indicates his wily, shifting character, but may also be linked with Treebeard's suggestion that Saruman has mingled the races of orcs and men which would be "a black evil" (p485) There are several references to the "blood of Numenor" which is symbolised by a white tree.

(If any Daily Mail readers chance upon this book, I am not denouncing Tolkien as a racist or insisting that The Lord of the Rings should be banned or burnt. I am just drawing attention to something anyone can read in the text for themselves.)

It is not primarily to racial prejudice that Tolkien is appealing but to a more basic fear – fear of the dark. Fear of darkness is instinctive. It is known to every child and it is sensible to assume that men have always feared the dark, which was a real source of danger to our ancestors. This is one of the reasons why the taming of fire (see Chapter 2) was so important. Religions – from Zoroastrianism to Christianity – have reflected these fears by using light and dark as symbols for good and evil.

Fear of darkness is primarily fear of the unknown. One of the ways in which this novel works is not by showing the reader horrors but by allowing us to guess at the nature of forces which remain wrapped in shadow. Thus the 'Lord of the Rings' of the title is never described. Isildur and Gollum both mention his hand and there are frequent references to his "evil eye" but there are no further details. The result of this is that the reader has no opportunity to domesticate this character. We never get close enough to see him eating or drinking or walking or talking. It is thus impossible to incorporate him into our experience of real people and we are forced to imagine someone so evil that he cannot be described.

Appendix A explains that Sauron had no bodily form but was "a spirit of hatred borne upon a dark wind" and his power "was through terror alone". The people of Gondor fear even to name Sauron or Mordor and frequent references to "The Shadow" seem to encompass both Sauron and his followers and the fear of Sauron.

Likewise the Nazgul - "the ringwraiths" - are invisible under their dark cloaks to all except Frodo (when he wears the Ring) They tend, rather like vampires, to prefer working at night. They are at their least powerful at mid-day. In the dark "they perceive many signs and forms that are hidden from us." (p206) The vampire image is enhanced by their dark flying steeds which resemble giant bats. Trolls, of course, are turned to stone by the rising sun. It is a sign of the growing power of the forces of darkness that Sauron has produced trolls who can withstand the sunlight (Appendix A)

As a result of Saruman's apparent genetic modification his orcs can operate in daylight. As we approach the climax of the novel the references to darkness increase in emphasis until at the very heart of Sauron's realm even the star-glass of Galadriel is unable to light the "stifling dark" (980)The darkest hour, as the old saw goes, is just before dawn. The growing power of evil, symbolised by the gathering gloom, precedes the overthrow of Sauron.

Darkness and shadows are also associated with death. In fact the Latin word "umbra" (echoed in the novel with the corsairs of Umbar with their black-sailed fleet) means both "shadow" and "ghost". Tolkien's use of names also suggests this link. Apart from the rather obvious "Dead Marshes" and "Mount Doom", "Gorgoroth" calls to mind "Golgotha" - place of the skull where Jesus was crucified. Mordor itself echoes the Latin "Morior" (to die) or "mordeo" (mortify) or more simply the English word "murder".

(Isaac Asimov uses the last of those facts in a short story (in "The Black Widowers")in which someone whose first language was not English overheard people discussing The Lord of the Rings and thought they were plotting a murder)

The gates of Minas Morgul which were "shaped like an open mouth with gleaming teeth" (p733) suggests the "Jaws of Hell" of the Miracle Plays. The "corpse-light", references to ghosts and haunting, the "maggot folk of Mordor", the "charnel smell" of the valley of the Ringwraiths (p73l) and many other references suggest this link.

Perhaps one of the most significant is the reference to the "valley of shadow and cold deadly light" (p732) which suggests the "valley of the shadow of death" (Psalm 23) because in this context the "shadow" refers to the fear of death rather than to death itself. Fear of death is a powerful source of evil in the novel. Numenor fell because men desired eternal life and one of the attractions of the Rings of Power offered to mortal men was that they offered eternal life. The achievement of the quest requires the conquest of that fear.

For the crusade against Sauron to succeed. Aragorn has to summon the shades of the dead to help him defeat the forces of the enemy. Gimli comments on this "strange and wonderful I thought it that the designs of Mordor should be overthrown by such wraiths of fear and darkness (my emphasis)F With its own weapons was it worsted." (p9l0)

However, the difference between Aragorn and Sauron (the Necromancer) in this is that Aragorn summons the restless spirits of the dead so that they can fulfil their oath and have peace. Sauron on the other hand, created wraiths which were kept alive beyond their due span until "every last minute is a weariness" (p60) Moreover the spirits Aragorn summons come of their own free will whereas the Nazgul and Sauron's other servants echo only his will.

It is interesting to note that on two occasions need drives members of the Company of the Ring underground. On both occasions there is one member who is forewarned of his own death but nevertheless continues. In both cases there is one member who is unwilling to go. Halbarad knew that his death lay on the paths of the dead and Gimli "dragged his feet like lead" over the threshold. Gandalf was warned of his peril if he passed the gates of Moria and Boromir entered against his will (p327)

All of this emphasises the need to overcome fear of darkness and death in order to triumph over evil. After the overthrow of Sauron, at the time of Aragorn's wedding to Arwen, Frodo remarks,

"This is the ending. Now not only day shall be beloved , but night too shall be beautiful and blessed and all its fear pass away!" (pl099)

Tolkien underscores this point by ending the novel with the peaceful passing over the "sundering sea" of the ringbearers. This contrasts strongly with the many violent deaths which the reader has witnessed. Death is referred to as "the gift of the One to Men" (Appendix A) and Aragorn's last words are - "but let us not be overthrown by the final test, who of old renounced the Shadow and the Ring. In sorrow we must go, but not in despair. Behold! We are not bound for ever to the circles of the world and beyond them is more than memory. Farewell!" (Appendix A)

Thus Aragorn renounced the "Shadow" - in this context I take this to mean fear of death. He renounced the Ring which apparently offered eternal life but would bind him to the "circles of the world." Arwen renounced both the Shadow and the twilight (Appendix A) The twilight suggests the eternal life of the elves who are associated with the eternal stars. Roy Calvert (a character in CP Snow's The Light and the Dark) was obsessed by fear of death. He said that he hated the stars because they did not die and seemed to be mocking him. I feel this is similar to the feelings of the Numenoreans towards the elves and illustrates the applicability of Tolkien's ideas to the human condition.

Jung's theory of archetypes in the collective unconscious suggests the Shadow may have a further meaning. For Jung, the Shadow was an archetype which "corresponds to a negative ego personality; it embraces all those characteristics whose existence is found to be painful or regrettable." (The Integration of the Personality p 173)

One interesting characteristic of the Shadow is that; "in a man's case the anima has a definitely feminine and the Shadow an equally definite masculine character." (ibid p2l) It should be noted that there are no evil female characters in the novel. I exclude Shelob from this because she is neutral between Sauron and the Westerners. (see Chapter 5 for more about this) The elves tend to have what are often thought of as female characteristics – slender and graceful forms and sweet voices. There are no female orcs presented.

Secondly, Jung suggests that when the shadow engulfs the ego, "the ego becomes more infantile". I am inclined to associate this with the fact that a Mortal who possesses a Great Ring "does not grow and obtain new life", in other words he (they are all male) does not develop maturity. We can see both Bilbo's and Frodo's reversion to egocentricity when anyone tries to take their "precious" Ring from them. Significantly they can no longer recognise their closest friends and they themselves become unrecognisable. Jung suggests this is one of the manifestations of possession of the ego by the shadow (ibid. p946)

A symbol of the engulfing of the ego by the Shadow is the invisibility (facelessness) of the Nazgul. Their nebulous existence and lack of individual will represents the final stage in a process of destruction of the personality which we can see in other characters. As Gandalf explains: "a mortal who uses one of the Great Rings … if he often uses it to make himself invisible, he fades: he becomes in the end invisible permanently, and walks in the twilight under the eye of the dark power which rules the Rings"(p60)

The loss of identity is apparent in Smeagol who says of himself: "poor Smeagol went away long ago." Another example is the "Mouth of Sauron" who has forgotten his own name (p922) It is significant that on the two occasions Frodo is released from evil influences he is himself again - "suddenly he was aware of himself again. Frodo, neither the voice nor the eye: free to choose and with one remaining instant in which to do it." (p42l) and "there was Frodo, pale and worn, and yet himself again." (p982)

Moreover, the concept of a Shadow which is not a thing in itself but an insubstantial dark distorted image of reality is an important factor in Tolkien's vision of evil. Although the imagery of light and dark is Zoroastrian in origin, Tolkien's use of it can be shown to be Christian although there are no overt Christian references in the novel itself. The shadow, we are told, "can only mock it cannot make."(p948), moreover, "Nothing is evil in the beginning, even Sauron was not so." (p283)

Zoroastrianism has a duallist approach. The forces of light (Ormazd) and darkness (Ahriman) are both seen as having an existence. Christianity, since St Augustine, has tended to see evil not as a separate entity but as the corruption, privation or perversion of something good. Christianity tends to equate existence with good. "In the beginning, God created the heaven and the earth" (Genesis I I) – thus at the heart of evil we find the shadow of non-existence. That is why Sauron's eye was "a window into nothing"(p383) Likewise, the windows of Minas Morgul looked "inward into emptiness" and when the Lord of the Nazgul was destroyed by Merry and Eowyn, "the mantle and hauberk were empty".

The final picture of the might of Sauron enhances this image:

"black against the pall of cloud, there rose a huge shape of shadow, impenetrable, lightning-crowed, filling all the sky. Enormous it reared above the world, and stretched out towards them a vast threatening hand, terrible but impotent: for even as it leaned over them, a great wind took it, and it was all blown away, and passed; and then a hush fell." (p985)

In the Silmarillion, Tolkien explains that, like Gandalf ("Olorin"), Sauron was originally one of the Maiar. He was corrupted by Melkor "and was only less evil than his master in that for long he served another and not himself. But in after years he rose like a shadow of Morgoth and a ghost of his malice, and walked behind him on the same ruinous path down to the Void." (Silmarillion p32) If we link this with Gandalf's challenge to the Lord of the Nazgul - "Fall into the nothingness that awaits you and your master." (p89l) we can see the working out of the Augustinian view that the corruption we call evil "is never complete, if a thing becomes so vitiated in nature that it ceases to exist the evil which is parasitic upon it must also cease to exist." (Contra Faust um Manichaeum)

Right up to the eucatastrophe – which is Tolkien's opposite of Wagner's Gotterdamerung – the Shadow appears to be immensely powerful like the "black threatening hand" of Sauron. Yet like the hand it is really impotent. Fear makes it larger than it really is - "he who flies counts every foeman twice." The main reason for this impotence is that malice is self-defeating (see Chapter 4)

The flame of Anor and the Flame of Udun

In the novel Tolkien presents two types of fire - the flame of Anor (the Sun) and the flame of Udun (Hell) This presentation emphasises a dichotomy in the connotation of the concept of fire. On the one hand we associate it with warmth, the domestic image of the hearth, the life-giving heat and light or the Sun, the cosy picture of the camp-fire in the wilderness as a centre for human community in a hostile environment. On the other hand we learn very early in life to fear fire and to associate it with pain. It is also a word we associate with wanton destruction and danger "Awake! Fire! Fear! Foes!" (pl92)

Thus Gandalf - "the keeper of the secret flame of Anor" - uses his power to create a fire which saves the company from perishing amidst the snows of Carathras, and uses fire as a weapon to defend the Company against the wargs. This emphasises the life-sustaining powers of the flame of Anor. The taming of fire was probably the first major conquest of man in the development of civilisation because it enabled physically weak creatures to warm themselves and defend themselves from wild beasts who were stronger than themselves. It should be noted that Smeagol's anti-social nature is emphasised by his preference for uncooked fish and meat, whereas Sam's joy in cooking helps to endear him to the reader. (p68l)

Aragorn uses fire to repel the Nazgul when they attack the company on Weathertop, and to combat the deadly chill which creeps over Frodo after he has been wounded with a Morgul knife. Significantly one of the orcs Frodo and Sam overhear in Mordor suggests that the Nazgul will "Freeze the flesh off" his companion (p96l) and when the Nazgul comes close to Frodo at the ford, "a breath of deadly cold pierced him like a spear." (p230) Also, the hobbits are tormented by the chill air of Mordor (p968)

It might be noted that in Milton's vision of Hell the damned are not only tormented by fire but

"Are brought and feel by turns the bitter change …
From Beds of raging Fire to starve in Ice"
(Paradise Lost Book 2 lines 598-600)

Thus extreme cold and destructive fire are both manifestations of evil, while the life-sustaining power of the flame of Anor is emphasised. On a more trivial level, Gandalf is remembered for his fireworks, for his pipe with which he blew such marvellous smoke-rings in The Hobbit. These details help to make this lofty wizard a more human and likeable character who was prepared to use his great powers purely for amusement, to entertain himself and others.

In contrast with the deadly chill of the Nazgul, we are presented with the fire-demon, the Balrog. From the Silmarillion we learn that "their hearts were of fire, but they were cloaked in darkness, and terror went before them: they had whips of flame." (p47) The conflict between the flame of Udun and the keeper of the flame of Anor is played out on the bridge of Khazad-dum (pronounced 'doom') It is full of pictures of red fire, called "ghash" by the orcs which is contrasted with Gandalf's white fire. For example:
"From out of the shadow a red sword leaped flaming.

"Glamdring glittered white in answer.

"There was a ringing clash and a flash of white flame. The Balrog fell back and its sword flew up in molten fragments."

I would suggest there are two reasons for this particular contrast. Firstly, white is associated with purity and red is associated with evil. In common parlance we talk about being "caught red handed", "scarlet shame" and of course "red for danger". (One of the things which may have been in Tolkien's mind is the struggle between the Reds and the Whites in Communist counties but I would put it no stronger than that)

Secondly white heat is more powerful than red. An example of Tolkien's metaphorical use of this can be seen in the battle of the Pelennor fields where the chieftain of the Haradrim was filled with a "red wrath" but the "white fury of the Northmen burned the hotter." (p973) and he was defeated.

In the conflict between Gandalf and the Balrog, the Balrog appears to drag Gandalf into the depths and thus defeat him but Gandalf actually survives and ultimately casts down his enemy. This shows a relationship between the flame of Anor and the flame of Udun which is repeated elsewhere in the novel. At the very heart of Sauron's realm stands Orodruin (it is no accident that Tolkien used the word "ruin" to signify "red flame") The red flame of Orodruin sends up a fume and a reek which blots out the life-giving fire of the Sun but is unable to destroy it.

Samwise, who bears the white flame of Galadriel close to his heart is able to look above the reek of Mordor and see "a white star twinkle for a while" and this leads him to reflect that "in the end the shadow was only a small and passing thing: there was light and high beauty forever beyond its reach." (p957) Although evil may appear mighty, the God-created universe is mightier still.

There are numerous examples of the use of fire to destroy life in the novel - in particular Saruman's destruction of Fangorn's trees to feed the fires of Isengard and the fire-bombing of Minas Tirith under the direction of the Lord of the Nazgul. However the "ruin" which evil brings has a wider significance in terms of the destruction of personality. This link is most clearly shown in the case of Denethor whose self-destructive pride and despair leads him to add to the destructive work of the orcs who are burning the first circle of Minas Tirith by bringing fire to the hallows of Rath Dinen. Denethor's statement about Faramir - who is "already burning" with fever - "The house of his spirit crumbles", is echoed in the collapse of the House of the Dead while his pyre rages within. The outward destructiveness of fire is the counterpart of the inward destruction of the spirit of Denethor. His statement about his son is more applicable to himself, but he is determined that his son should perish with him.

Like Saruman, Denethor's degeneration is linked to his use of a palantir. Tolkien's imagery closely links the palantir with destructive fire - "the globe began to glow with an inner flame, so that the lean face of the Lord was lit as with a red fire." (p887) It is interesting that Pippin - who has also looked in a palantir later says "Well, now at any rate I understand Denethor a little better. We might die together, Merry and I, and since die we must, why not." (p926)

The role of the palantiri highlights one of the themes of the novel – "Perilous to us all are the devices of an art deeper than we possess ourselves." (p62l) Tolkien is proposing, in mythological form, an idea which is extremely relevant to the modern world. Denethor was led to his pyre by probing the seeing stone and misinterpreting the truth which it showed him because his knowledge was incomplete. I am inclined to link this with the dwarves who sought truesilver in Moria, but delved too deep and awoke a Balrog. I have taken to heart Tolkien's warning about reading the novel as mere allegory but I think that an example of the truth Tolkien reveals could be the discovery of atomic power - having discovered this wonderful secret of nature man could think of nothing more sensible to do with it than to create a weapon of mass destruction - a veritable fire-demon - rather like a child playing with matches.

There is a similarity between the position of Denethor and the final position of Frodo on Mount Doom. Denethor has been steward of the realm of Gondor with the purpose of maintaining power in order to hand it over to the King, Frodo has been a "steward" of the Ring. Both are unwilling to relinquish their stewardship. In both cases the symbol of fire is used to indicate the destruction of personality, as the red flame of the palantir distorts Denethor's features, so the "wheel of fire" plays an important role in Frodo's journey into Mordor.

The symbol of the wheel of fire links together the symbols of the eye and the ring. This is a link which Tolkien also makes by his use of the expression "an orb of hot gold", since the word "orb" means both "ring" and "eye" among other things. The wheel itself is an interesting symbol. It is both a symbol of industry (see Chapter 6) and a symbol of torture – recalling the Medieval punishment of "breaking on the wheel". In this case it is not Frodo's body which is being broken but his spirit. Whereas Gandalf's battle with the Balrog shows the "literal struggle between the flame of Anor and the flame of Udun, Frodo's battle with the wheel of fire can be said to represent the metaphysical aspect of the struggle. In addition to the external torment of privation, weariness and thirst in the wasteland or dust and ashes, Frodo's spirit has to contend with the growing power of the evil desires which the ring represents and which he must renounce. At first he is troubled by dreams of fire, then he comes to see the wheel of fire with his waking eyes, and finally on the road to the cracks of Doom, Sam sees him as "a figure robed in white, but at its breast it held a wheel of fire. Out of the fire (my emphasis) there spoke a commanding voice." (p979)

On one level this "commanding voice" is simply the Ring warning Smeagol not to touch it again and thus protecting itself. On another level it is Frodo's burning desire to retain the Ring which is mastering his soul - "the figure robed in white". Although this evil desire masters Frodo on the brink of the cracks of Doom - where, significantly, Sam's white flame is also powerless - it is the flame of Anor which ultimately triumphs because of the pity shown by Frodo and Sam (and of course Bilbo) in sparing Smeagol's life.

The persuasive voice of evil

"The words of the wizard stand on their heads ... In the language of Orthanc help means ruin and saving means slaying." (p602)

The main struggle against the renegade Wizard Saruman begins and ends with the unmasking of dishonesty by Gandalf. Later, in the scouring of the Shire, the pattern is completed when the first unmasked villain (Wormtongue) murders the second unmasked villain (Saruman).

Although the Saruman story appears to be a diversion from the main plot, it in fact performs a number of functions. For my purposes its function is to explore an aspect of evil - the pleasant mask and persuasive voice which evil can adopt - which is not dealt with in such depth elsewhere.

The first traitor we encounter is the aptly-named Wormtongue who has "wormed" his way into Theoden's confidence and. has affected his spirit in much the same way as a woodworm affects a stout oak beam. His name also suggests the symbol of the worm which is associated with the symbol of the Serpent who tempted Adam and Eve with lies. It also suggests a spy who worms out secrets. This is one of Wormtongue's roles in Rohan.

We first see him spreading dissension and doubt in Theoden's golden hall and seeking to create disunity. He instructs the guards to admit none but those who speak their language and insists that no visitor should bear any weapon into the hall. The importance of these instructions is that they are quite sensible security precautions but they serve to create an atmosphere of distrust in which intrigue can flourish. He almost succeeds in creating a confrontation between Aragorn and the guards. Gandalf's intervention and Hama's common sense ("In doubt a man of worth will trust to his own wisdom." p534) defeat this particular ploy.

He next makes use of the ancient prejudice against a bearer of ill news to poison Theoden's mind against Gandalf and creates an impressionistic word picture of the world situation which is calculated to produce despair. Significantly everything that he says is true but he cleverly selects and slants his facts to create the desired impression. Gandalf dramatically illustrates what Wormtongue has been doing by causing the hall to become dark and then demonstrates that it is an illusion by persuading Theoden to look on the reality outside his doors - "It is not so dark here." (p538) - and at the same time demonstrating to him that age does not lie so heavily on his shoulders as Wormtongue would have him believe.

In the book and in the film, Theoden's triumph over old age and the fear of death is one of the most moving parts of the narrative. Or perhaps that's just my age talking!

It is significant that Gandalf exposes Wormtongue as soon as the latter strays from statements of fact and opinion about matters of which he has had experience to a statement about Dwimordene of which he can have had no experience. Our verbal representation of reality bears a varying relation to that reality. At times our symbols are transparent but they have a tendency to become opaque. It is this latter tendency which enables us to create a "reality" which has no factual existence - as Tolkien is doing in this novel. The source of Theoden's error was that he accepted Wormtongue's harsh word-picture of the situation as reality.

What Gandalf offers Theoden is not a new set of "facts" but a new way of looking at the situation. It is significant that his answer to Wormtongue is in verse (p536) and the public demonstration of Theoden's transformation is also in verse (p540) By entering into verse they enter a realm where Wormtongue can no more follow them than he could enter Dwimordene. The poetic truth which offers hope is contrasted with the prosaic "truth" which offers despair.

Wormtongue robs Theoden of his virility - a symbol' of this is that he deprives him of his sword. Theoden's virility is restored when his nephew and heir Eomer gives him his sword which Theoden then returns to him when he reinstates him in his position.

Wormtongue's last ditch attempt to retain his position takes the form of an appeal to conservatism - Theoden should defend Edoras rather than going forth to challenge Saruman. More particularly he appeals to Theoden to save his own life. Subsequently Theoden does die after he has witnessed the overthrow of Saruman and contributed to it and has felled "the black serpent" at the gates of Minas Tirith. However, this death is preferable to Wormtongue's leech craft which "ere long would have had me walking on all fours like a beast,"

.

Theoden achieves freedom because he is prepared to sacrifice his life and to risk sacrificing his "golden hall". Both Wormtongue and Saruman are offered freedom by Gandalf but are unable to make use of it. Saruman will not sacrifice Orthanc and Wormtongue is trapped with him until at the end of the novel the "worm" turns on his master for parading his subservience once too often. Even in this final act Wormtongue is imitating Saruman who has just made a treacherous attack on Frodo.

Saruman's voice is a sharp contrast from the voices of his orcs and other evil characters. It has the tone of "a kindly heart aggrieved by injuries undeserved," (p60l) as opposed to the harsh uncouth tones of Ugluk. He uses longer sentences, makes greater use of subordinate clauses and uses a wider vocabulary. In short, his speech has a more cultured and intelligent tone to it.

As a philologist, Tolkien was, of course, very conscious of the power of words. In 1958 he said, "I look East, West, North and South and I do not see Sauron; but I see that Saruman has many descendants." (J R R Tolkien: A Biography, H Carpenter p 228) I would not suggest that Saruman was based on any particular politician, newspaper proprietor or demagogue but that what is said about him gives us an insight into how they operate.

Saruman begins with elaborate flattery in his appeals to both Theoden and Gandalf and seeks to sow dissension between them. His treatment of Gimli and Eomer initially reveals the ugly side of his nature, but he cleverly suggests they are being disrespectful to Theoden in interrupting him. Theoden's reply shows his understanding of Saruman's method by saying one thing and meaning another "we will have peace" (which causes the riders under Saruman's spell to cheer "...when you and all your works have perished." (p603) The phrase "the devil and all his works" is evoked for many readers by this choice of words.

Saruman then reverses everything . The "worthy son of Thengel the thrice renowned" becomes a "dotard". His reference to Eomer's valour in arms becomes a reference to a "little band of gallopers, as swift to fly as to advance." (p604)

Saruman's nature is perhaps symbolised by his cloak which changed colour when he moved. This is both attractive and deceptive. The reality behind Saruman's sleek well-fed appearance is revealed after his death when "long years of death were suddenly revealed in it [his body] and the shrivelled face became rags of skin upon a hideous skull." (pl058) Another indication of the gap between appearance and reality is Saruman's symbol of the white hand, which appeared to be stained with blood as Gandalf passed it. (p579). Thus although Saruman's hand appears to be the opposite of Sauron's "black hand", it is not. Thus Theoden's metaphor: "You hold out your hand to me, and I perceive only a finger of the claw of Mordor." (p603) An outstretched hand is a symbol of peace, but not if it is "a finger of a claw" and a bloodstained one to boot!

The person who was most deceived by Saruman was Saruman himself. He "fondly imagined" that his cunning was creating something new, whereas in reality all he created was "a child's model or a slave's flattery" (p579) of Sauron's evil. As I have mentioned above, Tolkien makes clear that Sauron can only mock he cannot make. Thus Saruman's evil is only a copy of a copy. Like Melkor, or for that matter Satan, Saruman fell from grace through pride. "He will not serve only command." (p608)

The converse of the thesis that the practice of deception involves self-deception is that "the men of the Mark do not lie, and therefore they are not easily deceived." (p455) This is not strictly true since Wormtongue is a "man of the Mark" and so is Theoden whom he deceives. Nevertheless these theses are of interest. We notice that Saruman cannot understand Gandalf's motives and is therefore unable to deceive him. Likewise Sauron miscalculates because he cannot comprehend the disinterested motives which would lead his enemies to wish to destroy the Ring. In other words those whose minds are filled with cunning and trickery are incapable of understanding a straightforward honest motive.

Even Gandalf had to learn this lesson to some extent when he failed to perceive the simple answer to the problem of the dwarf-gates of Moria - "I had only to speak the Elvish word for 'friend' and the doors opened. Quite simple. Too simple for a learned lore master in these suspicious days." (p326). One can imagine Saruman standing before those gates for months contriving subtle solutions. Apart from any other considerations I should imagine that "friendship" would be the last concept to enter his head.

Hence Tolkien is implying that deception involves self-deception, the traitor betrays himself as well as others, whereas those who are honest can see through deception more or less instinctively; it seems fair but feels foul (pl87) because they lack the sophistication to be daunted by mere words. Thus Gimli was the first to see through Saruman and Hama was able to see the truth when Gandalf arrived at Meduseld.

This also draws attention to the distinction between "wisdom" and "cunning". Like Boromir, Saruman initially sought to use evil for good purposes. His fall from these high ideals illustrates the fallacy in the doctrine that the end justifies the means. The fallacy is that means frequently become ends. Thus from the pursuit of power to do good, Saruman fell into the pursuit of power itself. This is a vice which both Denethor and Saruman project onto Gandalf but which is only true of themselves. Apart from allowing subtle means to obscure and ultimately replace noble ends, the other distinction between wisdom and cunning is that the former relies on harnessing the forces of nature, the latter on destroying them and replacing them with "subtle devices" - I deal with this point elsewhere.

The final degeneration of Saruman is perhaps indicated by his adoption of the name "Sharkey". Abandoning his real name in favour of an orcish one suggests the final surrender of his personality to evil. The unpleasant connotations of the name are two-fold, firstly it suggests a deadly animal whose main weapon is its mouth - which is appropriate enough. Secondly it calls to mind the slang use of "shark" to denote a small-time confidence trickster.

Oft Evil Will Shall Evil Mar

The idea that "Evil will shall evil mar" (p6l8) is repeated a number of times in the novel and it is a concept which plays an important role in Tolkien's plot. Thus Gandalf says of Smeagol , "A traitor may betray himself and do good that he does not intend" (p847) which could be a description of the unconscious good performed by both Smeagol and Saruman and even Sauron himself.

The victory of the Rohirrim at the battle of the Pelennor fields is a decisive turning point. Eomer says of the darkness created in Mordor - "Our Enemy's devices oft serve us in his despite. The accursed darkness itself has been a cloak to us." It would be tedious to catalogue all the examples of this idea in the novel, but I feel that the main lessons can be drawn from examining its significance in the Ringbearer's journey into Mordor itself.

Thus Frodo and Sam enter Mordor "aided" unconsciously by Smeagol's treachery. Without his knowledge of Cirith Ungol , they would not have been able to pass the Ephel Duath. At this stage also the lust of the orcs for Frodo's mail shirt leads them to internecine strife. Later Smeagol's small crime of stealing Frodo's discarded mail shirt puts the orc trackers off the track - and thus serves the Quest.

Thus we can say that one simple explanation of the marring of evil by evil will is the substitution of a lesser and immediately visible evil for a greater one. This is most clearly seen in Smeagol's two attacks on Frodo on Mount Doom itself. The first time he seeks to take the Ring this has the beneficial effect of awakening the "dying embers of Frodo's heart and will". (p978). His second attack causes the destruction of both the Ring and himself. All Smeagol can see in the situation is that Frodo has the Ring and "we wants it, we wants it!" and in his single-minded gloating over his success he falls into the Crack of Doom.

A related concept is that malice is self-defeating. Thus Wormtongue's attempt to kill Saruman places the Palantir in Aragorn's hands. This enables Aragorn to distract Sauron's attention from the two spies in his own land. Smeagol is "misled by spite" and thus "made the mistake of speaking and gloating before he had both hands on his victim's neck." (p754) and that is why he failed to kill Sam. Moreover Sauron was so intent on crushing the Lords of the West that he failed to notice Frodo and Sam until it was too late and concentrated all his forces in Udun, thus clearing their path to the mountain. In another sense the "spirit of Mordor" aids the Quest. The hatred which Sauron has encouraged in his slaves is extended to each other and to himself and is therefore self-defeating - the battle between Shagrat and Gorbag and the fight between the two hunters pursuing Frodo and Sam demonstrate this. Moreover the fear of Sauron prevents Shagrat reporting the capture of Frodo immediately - "It won't sound too pretty to say that you've caught the kitten and let the cat escape." (p768).

History is full of examples of authoritarian regimes which have fallen precisely because fear of the tyrant caused his servants to hide the truth from him. For example Hitler organised the last defence of Germany by deploying units and divisions which no longer existed but his staff had not dared to tell him of their destruction.

However, I think that Tolkien saw the main reason for evil's self-defeating nature was it's narrowed vision and egocentricity (perhaps represented by Sauron having but one eye). This can be seen from Gandalf's explanation of the situation -

"He supposes that we are all going to Minas Tirith; for that is what he would himself have done in our place (my emphasis). And according to his wisdom it would have been a heavy stroke against his power ... That we should wish to cast him down and have no one in his place is not a thought that occurs to his mind."

Thus the very sources of Sauron's strength - his single-minded will to power, the brutality and hatred of his orcs, the treachery of Smeagol and Saruman - can all be seen to be weaknesses which lead to his downfall. The final irony is the destruction of the Ring which would have enabled him to rule the world which causes the downfall of Barad dur.

It is very satisfying, both in the novel and in real life, to see the "engineer hoist with his own petard." As I have explained above, it also indicates the existence of forces beyond those we see. The idea of a "Ring of Doom" echoes the idea of a "Wheel of Fortune" which casts down the mighty Sauron from his seat and exalts the humble and meek halflings Frodo and Samwise.

The role of nature

"I am not altogether on anybody's side, because nobody is altogether on my side, if you understand me: nobody cares for the woods as I care for them ... there are some things, of course, whose side I am altogether not on ... these orcs and their masters." (pp493-4)

During their quest, the company of the Ring encounter various personified primitive forces of nature which either aid or thwart them. They are hindered by Old Man Willow in the Old Forest, by Caradhras and Shelob. They are aided by Tom Bombadil and by the Ents. In the latter category we might place the Woses who aid the riders of Rohan in order to retain their freedom.

Like Treebeard (quoted above) these forces are not altogether on anybody's side, but act to preserve their own interests. Thus both the Old Forest and Fangorn merely react against those who have chopped down and burnt trees. In one case this was hobbits, in the other it was orcs. It should be remembered that Fangorn comes close to killing Merry and Pippin before he hears their voices. There is an element of truth in Saruman's propaganda (as there is in all effective propaganda) - "You may find the Shadow of the Wood at your own door next: it is wayward and senseless, and does not love Men." (p603)

Tolkien explained that Tom Bombadil was originally intended to represent "the spirit of the (vanishing) Oxford and Berkshire countryside," (Carpenter p65) and in the novel he is identified with Ea - the earth. The definition of Ea - "It is" is similar to Goldberry's "explanation" of Tom - "He is" (p39). His reaction to the Ring could be taken - inter alia - as a metaphor for the relationship between evil and nature. The Ring, which is a symbol for evil, does not cause him to disappear which would be to lose his identity. Moreover he alone can see Frodo when the latter wears the Ring. Gandalf makes an important distinction when it is suggested that Tom has power over the Ring - "Say rather that the Ring has no power over him. He is his own master. But he cannot alter the Ring itself, nor break its power over others." (p283) If he were given the Ring to preserve it he would probably throw it away or lose it.

Thus nature can be seen to be morally neutral. Not concerned with evil and, in the final analysis, unable to resist it - "Sauron can torture and destroy the very hills." (p283) I take this to mean that the concept of evil, is man-made - it has no existence in nature but was called into existence by Man eating of the tree of knowledge of good, and evil (Genesis 3, 5) However, in the novel this does not prevent nature from being cruel or kind.

There is a primitive type of thinking, which Piaget called "animistic", which involves attributing intentions to forces and objects which have no intentions - "the carpet tripped me up". This is incorporated into our everyday language - we talk about the wind "blowing'" etc. Thus when Tolkien writes about a mountain "defeating" climbers or a forest misleading travellers, he is appealing to our most basic fears which have come down to us from our ancestors who probably really thought in this way. This is partly a result of the fact that the novel draws on traditional folklore.

An example of the destructive side of nature is Caradhras which "was called the Cruel, and had an ill name long ago, when rumour of Sauron had not been heard, in these lands." (p307). Another is Shelob (the name is a combination of she and lob, indicating a female spider) whom Sauron called "his cat" but "she owned him not". She is certainly 'neutral' in the sense that she would as soon devour an orc as a hobbit - "Little she knew or cared for towers, or rings, or anything devised by mind or hand, who only desired death for all others, mind and body, and for herself a glut of life." (p75l)

The animals harnessed by different sides in the war are distinctive - thus Sauron and Saruman make use of carrion crows, wolves, vampire bats and similar unlovely creatures whereas the Company of the Ring enlist the aid of loyal ponies, beautiful horses and, of course, the noble eagles. The last named is a particularly apt bird because it is a symbol of the Roman Catholic Church. This may have been one of the factors in Tolkien's choice.

Moreover the method of harnessing these animals is distinctive. Thus for example Gandalf's horse Shadow-fax - "is willing to carry you - or not. If he is willing, that is enough." (p620). Likewise Legolas requires neither saddle nor rein to solicit the co-operation of Arod. On the other hand Sauron makes use of "beasts spell-enslaved" (p985) and the horses of the Nazgul are stolen from Rohan or "born and bred to the service of the Dark Lord in Mordor." (p238) as were the Nazgul's unpleasant aerial steeds. Thus although nature can be compelled to serve evil purposes, it must be co-operated with to achieve good.

Water is frequently used in the novel to wash away evil. The dark riders were unhorsed by the river Bruinen, Isengard is washed clean with the waters of the Isen and rain lashes down on both Isengard and Mordor after the defeats of Saruman and Sauron respectively. This recalls the waters of baptism washing away our sins.

Similarly the West wind disperses the shadow of Mordor and destroys the "dark figure" of Sauron as it does the "grey figure" of Saruman. However we have only to recall the passage of the Dead Marshes to realise that water, wind

and rain are not always a blessing. Nevertheless I feel that Tolkien's use of the wind and the rain to "celebrate" the downfall of evil does suggest a certain harmony between the forces of Good and Nature.

.

Dark Satanic Mills

"Here nothing "lived, not even the leprous growths that feed on rottenness. The gasping pools were choked with ash and crawling muds, sickly white and grey, as if the mountains had vomited the fifth of their entrails upon the lands about. High mounds of crushed and powdered rock, great cones of earth fire-blasted and poison-stained, stood like an obscene graveyard in endless rows, slowly revealed in the reluctant light." (p657)

This dramatic word-picture of the desolation which lay before Mordor underlines one of the themes of the novel: the contrast between the beauties of nature and the rural life and the ugliness arising from industrialisation. The images of sickness - "gasping", "choked", "sickly", "vomited" are reinforced with images of violence - "crushed and blasted" and with images suggesting death - "graveyard", "poison" etc. This is reinforced with hyperbole - "as if the mountains had vomited the filth of their entrails" and the "reluctant light" suggesting that the sun itself was horrified by the sight.

Tolkien paints the blackest possible picture of the worst aspects of the industrial revolution - the dirt, the destruction of beautiful landscapes with ugly slag heaps, the smoke billowing from factory chimneys, the enslavement of vast numbers of people.

In the novel this is sharply contrasted with the idyllic scenes of - say - the great rolling grasslands of Rohan and the cosy rustic life of the Shire. This contrast is reinforced by the proximity of beauty and ugliness. The reader moves abruptly from Rohan to Isengard, from the gates of Mordor to fair Ithilien, from Sharkey's Shire to a scoured Shire.

The first example of industrialisation that we come across is that of Saruman who has "a mind of metal and wheels and does not care for growing things." (p494) He employs orcs to cut down trees in Fangorn to feed the fires of Isengard. Every green thing within the walls of Isengard is destroyed by the process of industrialisation for military purposes. Pillars of metal line the avenues as if in mockery of the trees which were destroyed in their forging and the circle of Isengard is undermined by forges and furnaces which pollute the environment with foul fumes.

Nature's revenge on Saruman is carried out by the Ents. Carpenter records that Tolkien remembered "the bitter disappointment and disgust from schooldays with the shabby use made in Shakespeare of the coming of Great Burnham Wood to high Dunsinane Hill': I longed to devise a setting in which the trees might really march to war." (Carpenter p35)

Tolkien's almost obsessive love of trees can be seen in his introduction to "Tree and Leaf" where he explains that one of the sources of "Leaf by Niggle" was "a great-limbed poplar tree that I could see even lying in bed. It was suddenly lopped and mutilated by its owner, I do not know why. It is cut down now, a less barbarous punishment for any crimes it may have been accused of, such as being large and alive. I do not think it had any friends, or any mourners, except myself and a pair of owls." The tree is an ancient symbol of life - our use of Christmas trees is a distorted remembrance of Odin's sacred oak. Thus the march of the Ents can be seen as a rebellion of the forces of life against industrialisation, which is not only inhuman but hostile to all forms of life.

The other force of nature which contributes to Saruman's destruction is the River Isen which is used to flood Isengard. Purification by water is also suggested in relation to the wasteland before the Morannon but significantly this is referred to as "a lasting monument to the dark labours of its slaves that would endure when all their purposes were made void." (p657) It would take "the Great Sea" (p657) to wash away the filth of Sauron, but a river suffices for Saruman. This stresses the point that he is merely imitating Sauron and the imitation is a pale one.

As I have mentioned above, the source of evil in Saruman was his substitution of cunning for wisdom. He had "long studied the arts of the Enemy himself." (p275) From studying evil in order to combat it he turned to practising it. He thought (or at least said) that by allying themselves with Sauron, the Wise could ultimately come to direct his policies, "deploring maybe evils done by the way, but approving the high and ultimate purposes; Knowledge, Rule, Order." (p277) His reliance on "subtle devices" led to a waning of his own personality and hence his real power. Without his precious machinery he has "not much plain courage alone in a tight place" (p590). Thus he is unable to deal with the forces of nature which he has left out of his calculations.

Mordor itself is an arid wasteland. Nothing grows - except some very thorny bushes which Sam encounters while fleeing the Nazgul (p952). The water is "at once bitter and oily" (p956). In Gorgoroth, "smokes trailed on the ground and lurked in hollows, and fumes leaked from fissures in the earth." (p958). Thus earth, air, fire and water are all polluted.

Tolkien places at the heart of Sauron's realm, "the forges of his ancient might, greatest in Middle Earth", within the mountain there is a "rumour and trouble as of great engines throbbing and labouring." (p980). This emphasises how central to Tolkien's vision of evil industry was.

The example which "brings it home" to the reader is the mill at Hobbiton, which Tolkien explicitly links with the "shabby destruction" of the British countryside in the foreword (pl0).

"Pimple knocked it down almost as soon as he came to Bag End. Then he brought in a lot of dirty-looking men to build a bigger one and fill it full of wheels and outlandish contraptions. Only that fool Ted was pleased by that, and he works there cleaning wheels for the Men, where his dad was the Miller and his own master. Pimple's idea was to grind more and faster, or so he said. He's got other mills like it. But you've got to have grist before you can grind; and there was no more for the new mill to do than for the old. But since Sharkey came they don't grind no more corn at all. They're always a-hammering and a-letting out a smoke and a stench, and there isn't no peace even at night in Hobbiton. And they pour out filth a purpose; they've fouled all the lower Water, and it's getting down into Brandywine. If they want to make the Shire a desert, they're going the right way about it." (pl050).

In the first place we have, as with Saruman, a good intention - "to grind more and faster" but one which ignores the laws of nature - "you've got to have grist before you can grind," The unnaturalness is emphasised by the interruption of the natural rhythms of rural life by the introduction of night-work and the loss of freedom and independence by Ted Sandman. A happy slave is a rather more pathetic sight than a miserable one.

One of the consequences of industrialisation was to make man the servant of the machine rather than its master. Sandyman represents the beginning of a process of which the orcs - who in some respects resemble H G Wells' Morlocks, degenerate work-beasts - are the final result.

Again the symbol of the wheel - an echo of Saruman's "mind of metal and wheels" (p494) - is used. The wheel was probably the first major "technological change" in the lives of men, but here they are kept turning for no intelligible purpose -"they don't grind no more corn at all." All Sharkey's factories produce is pollution and misery. This calls to my mind the picture of the treadmill as a symbol of useless and never-ending toil.

Thus Tolkien gives a purely negative - an enemy might say "luddite" - picture of industry. The machine weakens and demoralises he whom it serves (Saruman) and causes those who serve it to degenerate. It wantonly destroys the countryside and fouls earth air and water. Where it has any purpose at all, it is the pursuit of power - either the forging of weapons or the Ring of Power itself.

The Ring of Power

"All power tends to corrupt and absolute power corrupts absolutely" (Lord Acton).

Lord Acton's pithy little aphorism undoubtedly constitutes one of the themes of the book. This finds its clearest expression in relation to the Ring of Power and the effect it has on those who desire it.

Perhaps the clearest example of this is the case of Boromir. Boromir is a rather proud and haughty character. His remark on Caradhras - "But happily your Caradhras has forgotten, that you have Men with you. And doughty Men too, if I may say it," is rather typical of his boastful nature. It should be noted, however, that at least his boasts are truthful.

Although brave and honourable, his objectives differ from the rest of the Company in that he wishes firstly to overthrow Sauron as the age-old enemy of Minas Tirith and also to defend and extend the power of Minas Tirith.

Thus the source of Boromir 's error is the pursuit of sectional interests at the expense of more general considerations and, once again, the concept that "the end justifies the means".

My impression of Boromir is as of a simple soldier who has got out of his depth. The Wise renounce certain victory by the use of evil methods in favour of a slim chance of overthrowing the Enemy by non-military methods. This is too subtle for him. Ironically he says: "True-hearted Men, they will not be corrupted." (p4l8) at the very time when his corruption by the Ring becomes apparent.

In the very forging of the Ring we have another example of a noble purpose - the pursuit of knowledge by the elven smiths of Eregion - perverted to evil consequences. They accepted the assistance of Sauron, who in turn learned all their secrets and betrayed them.

One of the consequences of possession of the Ring was longevity. This was also true of the "Nine for Mortal Men doomed to die" although it was not true of the Seven or the Three.

I use the term longevity rather than immortality as the Lord of the Nazgul was killed by Merry while still wearing his ring and Deagol was killed while holding the One Ring.

We are told by Faramir (p704) that the search for eternal life unchanging was the source of the decline of the Numenoreans. Thus the fear of death can be seen as one of the ways in which evil comes into the world. It is significant that Arwen renounces her immortality for the love of Aragorn and this act ensures that the line of Elendil can continue. Thus - to put it baldly - love conquers death (or at any rate the fear of death). It should be noted that the eternal life offered by the Ring is a fraud - "A mortal, Frodo, who keeps one of the Great Rings, does not die, but he does not grow or obtain new life, he merely continues, until at last every minute is a weariness" (p60). Thus, for example, Bilbo did not feel "well-preserved" but "thin and stretched" (p45).

The Ring is "precious". Gollum/Smeagol uses this term most frequently, but it also crops up in Isildur's description of the Ring (p270) and acts as a warning to Gandalf when it is used by Bilbo (p46). Some light is thrown on the significance of this by Aragorn's comment, in another context, that "One who cannot cast away a treasure at need is in fetters." (p587). The triumph of Good over Evil requires sacrifice of that which is most precious to us. This can apply both to material possessions and possibly life itself.

Tolkien closely associates the Ring with the image of the Evil Eye. Bilbo says "Sometimes I have felt it was "like an eye looking at me." (p47) The lidless (i.e. sleepless) eye is a symbol of Sauron. Even the flies in Mordor are marked with "a red eye-shaped blotch." (p956)

Frodo's first sight of the Eye comes when he looks in the Mirror of Galadriel - "In the black abyss there appeared a single Eye that slowly grew, until it nearly filled the Mirror. So terrible was it that Frodo stood rooted, unable to cry out or to withdraw his gaze. The Eye was rimmed with fire, but was itself glazed, yellow as a cat's, watchful and intent, and the black slit of its pupil opened on a pit, a window into nothing." (p383)

This vision is associated with the Ring which grew heavier as Frodo watched. Almost immediately afterwards it is revealed that Frodo's vision is greater than he thought because he not only sees the ring on Galadriel's finger but also perceives her secret desire for the One Ring.

The reference to the "abyss" and the "pit" in the description of the Eye are reminders of the bottomless pit of Hell. This image is enhanced by the mention of the "rim of fire" which is later echoed in the "wheel of fire" and in this context is a reminder of the "fire and brimstone" of the medieval vision of Hell.

The cat was a traditional familiar of witches (from which our superstitions concerning black cats arises) and has a "slit" rather than a circular pupil which does lend it a sinister aspect. Cats also have better night vision than we do, being nocturnal hunters, and their eyes appear to glow in the darkness. Thus Tolkien's description takes us from the known to the unknown. The eye of Sauron can see in the darkness and never sleeps. Whereas the Ring renders the wearer invisible to most eyes, it renders him uniquely visible to its evil creator.

The eye is the only part of Sauron we actually see, although we have"hearsay evidence"from Smeagol and Isildur about his hand. The eye provides us with a good deal of information. The eye was thought to be the mirror of the soul – for example, Gandalf could tell from Pippin's eyes whether he was telling the truth (p6l6).

.

The evil eye is something we have all heard of "like a shadow on the borders of old stories" so to speak. Our superstitions concerning cross-eyed people have their origin in a belief that certain people had the power to cause harm to others by a look. Hypnosis – the domination of one will by another – was once thought to proceed from the eyes of the hypnotist. There is an element of truth in this. When animals or humans confront each other, it is he who is first to lower his eyes who is vanquished - fear of the Evil Eye probably originated in this natural custom.

Rings of power - both in myth and reality - have a long history. Romans wore rings as a badge of citizenship and the "signet ring" of a Medieval baron was literally"a "ring of power" which was used to give his seal of approval. Wagner's "Ring" cycle draws on ancient Nordic myths in its presentation of a golden ring which would give the wearer lordship of the earth.

However, the plain golden ring in the novel most closely resembles the wedding ring. The wedding ring originated, not as a ring of power but as a ring of bondage. It symbolised the chain which bound a female slave to her master's will, a chattel to her owner.

Thus the function of the Ring is twofold. On the one hand it is a ring of power - or would be in the hands of a Gandalf, a Galadriel or an Aragorn. On the other hand it tends to subject the wearer to the will of Sauron. However, as Gandalf hints "there are other forces at work", such as caused the ring to fall into Bilbo's hands.

Thus the Ring slips onto Frodo's finger against his will in the Inn at Bree. Although this exposes the ring-bearer and lays him open to attack by the Nazgul, it also draws him to the attention of Strider who rescues him. Although the Ring makes Sam uniquely visible in Mordor, it also gives the orcs a distorted picture of his strength and thus assists in the rescue of Frodo.

The Ring has less evil effect on Frodo than on Smeagol for a number of reasons. Firstly, he did not acquire it by force or treachery. Secondly he uses it very little and never for any evil purpose. Thirdly, and most importantly, he does not desire power or domination over others.

The same is true of Sam, who bears the Ring for a short while, "The one small garden of a free gardener was all his need and due, not a garden swollen to a realm; his own hands to use, not the hands of others to command." Thus Sam is saved from temptation because he is a good servant who "knows his place". The intrusion of the everyday subject of gardening into his deep deliberations has a threefold significance. It emphasises that it is his "plain hobbit sense" (p935), the fact that he is "down to earth", which saves him. Secondly it is another example of Tolkien using the familiar to explain the unfamiliar - we may never have to wrestle with Sam's temptations but we all know what gardening is about. Thirdly it suggests the importance of "original innocence" - according to Christian mythology we are all descended from a pair of gardeners who fell from grace after eating of the tree of knowledge of good and evil.

The word "free" in this context seems to denote not freedom from domination by others but freedom from the desire to dominate others. The point is, I think, that it comes to the same thing. In this context, as Sam says, Sauron would spot him and cow him immediately. In the wider context, we have seen that the Wise believed that the master of the Ring would cease to be his own master and become like Sauron.

Thus we have seen that the magic of the Ring is illusory. The long life it brings, the invisibility and the power of domination turn out to be a living death, a unique visibility and a form of slavery.

Its other powers, which are revealed to Sam, are of the same sort "The world changed, and a single moment of time was filled with an hour of thought. At once he was aware that hearing was sharpened while sight was dimmed, but otherwise than in Shelob's lair. All things about him now were not dark but vague; while he himself was there in a grey hazy world, alone, like a small black solid rock, and the Ring, weighing down his left hand, was like an orb of hot gold."

The time distortion would be very pleasant in, say, Ithilien. In Mordor one could wish it reversed. It emphasises the nightmare quality of the situation, which is enhanced by the "grey distorted figures in a mist" (p762) which the orcs become to Sam. It is interesting that with so much time for thought, Sam has time to become afraid - "he thought only of hiding, of lying low until all was quiet again." (p762) "Thus the native hue of resolution is sicklied o'er with the pale cast of thought."

His improved powers of hearing also deceive him as he misjudges how close he is to the orcs when he does summon up the pluck to attack them. However, Sam's delay in attacking turns to his advantage as the orcs start killing each other.

An interesting detail is that the Ring always goes on the left hand. Black Magic is often referred to as the "left hand path". Left-handedness being unusual there are a number of superstitions associating it with witchcraft, homosexuality and anything else unorthodox. In heraldry the "bar sinister" represents bastardy and our modern use of the word "sinister" suggests these connotations.

The "will to power" is a human characteristic which Nietzsche saw as inimical to Christianity. He saw Christianity as a "slave morality" which exalted such virtues as "turning the other cheek" and suggested that "the meek shall inherit the earth" because such were the hallmarks of a subject class or race and thus it satisfied their will to power in a distorted way by placing them above their oppressors. I submit that in the final resolution of Tolkien's "eucatastrophe" we can see a working out of the reverse of Nietzsche's view. Frodo's kindness to Smeagol is a weakness in Nietzschean terms, but Tolkien shows it to be a source of strength. Smeagol's will to power leads him to seize the Ring from Frodo and thus bring about his destruction and the destruction of his "precious". Sauron's will to power led him to create the "One Ring to rule them all" and it led to his downfall. Thus the climax of the novel can be seen as a triumph of the meek, symbolised by Frodo casting away his sword and the twice-repeated sparing of Smeagol by Frodo and Sam.

We could hardly ask for a greater contrast with Nietzsche's Superman than Smeagol. Whereas Tolkien shows us what a wise and powerful man may become if degraded by pride and the lust for power in his presentation of Saruman; with Smeagol he shows us what a person of smaller "stature" may become. In one sense the contrast favours Smeagol... "He had proved tougher than even one of the Wise would have guessed, as a hobbit might. There was a little corner of his mind that was still his own" (p68) .

Whereas desire for the Ring corrupted Saruman completely, Smeagol who actually possessed the Ring still retained some of his personality and he seems to come closer to redemption on the stairs of Cirith Ungol than Saruman does. His friendly gesture towards Frodo (p742) is misinterpreted by Sam because the latter has yet to learn pity for Smeagol by bearing the Ring himself.

The degrading nature of the will to power is emphasised by Gollum's animal characteristics - his preference for raw meat and fish, walking on all fours (p654) the preponderance of sibilants in his speech (suggesting a snake) etc - and by the use of animal imagery - "spider-like" (p742 and 637) "whipped cur" (p643)"frog-like" (p7l2) "wriggling like an eel, biting and scratching like a cat" (p7l5). Most of the animals suggested are unpleasant, particularly the spider which is used just before the meeting with Shelob and prepares the mind of the reader for the horror to come.

The suggestion of a snake is an image used throughout the novel in connection with evil - even the three "S"s of Sauron, Saruman(or Sharkey) and Smeagol suggest hissing. Snakes are usually thought of as a poisonous, slippery and slimy creatures symbolising Satan in Christian mythology. The numerous "dog'" references, particularly in "The Taming of Smeagol", while still derogatory, suggest a potentially tame and loyal creature.

Tolkien suggests the two sides of his nature by two names and two modes of speech. "Gollum" is a noise made in his throat which perhaps suggests the call of a bullfrog, but contains some suggestion of crying which elicits some sympathy from the reader.

His hissing speech is among the few examples of non-standard English in the novel which suggests an uncouth character and is midway between the common down-to-earth talk of hobbits like Sam and the ugly tongue of Mordor. Smeagol is not a very pleasant name - Sam calls this side of Gollum "Slinker" and it suggests words like "sneak" and "smarmy" to me. It should be remembered that Smeagol - not Gollum - murdered Deagol. Smeagol is not exactly Gollum's "good side" but his "real self". Smeagol does not use the egocentric speech of Gollum but speaks directly to his companions and uses the word "I". As I have suggested elsewhere, the regaining of personality means regaining the ability to choose Good or Evil. The egocentric Gollum could not choose to do good because his only frame of reference was his precious self. Sharing the companionship of Frodo and Sam widens Smeagol's frame of reference and awakens his potential for socio-centric choice which is almost realised on the stairs of Cirith Ungol.

.

Conclusion

I think the best way to summarise Tolkien's concept of Evil would be to make use of the aphorisms,which are usually put into Gandalf's mouth and could be said to contain ancient wisdom.

"The treacherous are ever distrustful" (p606).Throughout the novel, the distrust between say Saruman and Sauron and the trust between,say Aragorn and Eomer,are contrasted and demonstrate a strength of good and a weakness of Evil. I was interested to see that Paul Tocher in"The Master of Middle Earth" (p65) talks about the orcs having a "firm loyalty" which binds them to Sauron, yet the novel itself says that Sauron "had few servants but many slaves of fear" (p934) and the first conversation which Sam overhears between Gorbag and Shagrat shows their hatred and fear of the "big bosses, even the biggest" (p765).

In the novel the orcs are usually seen as an undifferentiated mass, but when we come closer to them we encounter a complete lack of mutual trust - Grishnakh and Ugluk, Gorbag and Shagrat and the two hunters Frodo and Sam encounter in Mordor, fall out and fight. Frodo comments, "That is the spirit of Mordor and it has spread to every corner of it." (p96l). Disunity outside Mordor also plays into the hands of the Enemy, the distrust between elves and dwarves (which Gimli and Legolas learn to overcome while fighting the common enemy), the "loyalty divided in a confusion of hearts" which Gandalf encounters in Minas Tirith (p885), the distrust engendered by the lies of Wormtongue in Rohan – all illustrate the problem.

The solution could be said to lie in the idea expounded by Hama: "In doubt a man of worth will trust to his own wisdom." (p534) Although Hama has no "scientific" evidence to support his trust, there is nevertheless something within himself which tells him to trust Gandalf. The fact that this aphorism comes from a minor character emphasises the fact that faith is the wisdom of simple and ordinary folk which learned loremasters such as Saruman or even Gandalf before the gates of Moria (see Section 3) may have lost.

"A traitor may betray himself and do good that he does not intend," (p847) is really a continuation of the above idea. It emphasises that however powerful evil may appear to be, it does not actually have an independent existence. This is because the Shadow "can only mock, it cannot make." (p948) In the final analysis the discord which evil creates only serves to add to the beauty of the "great music" which Tolkien uses as an analogy for God's creation.

"He that breaks a thing to find out what it is has left the path of true wisdom." (p276) This can be linked with the idea that "Nothing was evil in the beginning," and can be seen to have several layers of meaning. The vision of Saruman "of many colours" reminds us that evil can be very attractive. However Gandalf perceives that in trying to improve on his original whiteness Saruman is passing through the spectrum from white to black. At a deeper level I think that Tolkien is talking about the origins of evil. Man is unique in nature in his ability to categorise reality through the medium of language. The categories which we use have no existence in nature itself. They give rise to a higher abstraction from reality in formal Aristotelian logic. Hegel described this as "the source of all our knowledge and the source of all our error." This is because it deals with what is real for our representation of reality but not reality itself. Thus in this process of categorising, men, especially wise men, can fall into the trap of "not seeing the wood for the trees" (quite literally in Saruman's case). Thus evil, in Tolkien's vision, is not differentiated from good in nature, but Man calls it into existence by breaking it up in order to see what it is.

"One who cannot cast away a treasure at need is in fetters." (p587) is a phrase which recalled to my mind Marley's ghost dragging his chain of cash boxes through eternity. The theme of renouncing treasures runs throughout the book, Frodo and Sam leaving the comfort of Bag End is contrasted with Saruman's refusal to leave Orthanc. Sam casting away his treasured cooking utensils and, of course the climax of the Quest where Frodo is unable to relinquish the Ring. This is yet another echo of Christian teaching: "Lay not up for yourselves treasures upon earth,where moth and rust doth corrupt, and where thieves break through and steal: but lay up for yourselves treasures in Heaven, where neither moth nor rust doth corrupt, and where thieves do not break through and steal. For where your treasure is, there will your heart be also." (Matthew 6, l9-2l) The emphasis on renunciation underscores the importance of free will. The impulse to renounce worldly possessions must come from within because it is only in this way that the fetters which bind us to them may be broken because those fetters reside in our own will.

.

Thus in the end evil is involved with the "doom of choice". Although many aspects of the novel suggest the existence of divine providence, nevertheless the choices which individuals make are the decisive factor – especially the choices of Frodo and Sam, who are the smallest and weakest creatures in the novel, at least on the surface.

Although Frodo, for example, is tempted to use his own weakness and the Enemy's strength as an excuse, he chooses not to do so.

In real life we often blame objective circumstances for evil actions. We hear every day about "deprived home circumstances" or "adverse social conditions" forcing people to behave in an evil way as if they were not human beings capable of making choices. Any belief in the soul must seek the origin of evil not just in the environment but in our free will. Excusing the trespasses of others by reference to the objective circumstances is one thing. It is something Jesus enjoins us to do. Excusing ourselves is another.

When confronted with the temptation to do evil we are in the same position as Frodo "Suddenly he was aware of himself again. Frodo, neither the voice nor the eye: free to choose and with one remaining instant in which to do it."

The End

Postscript

When I wrote this I was not a Roman Catholic. Since then I have been baptised. My father always told me that it would be up to me to take the decision about being baptised. He probably didn't expect me to wait until I was sixty. I may have lost faith in God for a number of years. God never lost faith in me.

Amor Vincit Omnia

Also by the author

If you enjoyed this, you will also enjoy the other books in the #mirrorofeternity series.

Stories from the Mirror of Eternity

This is the first in the #mirrorofeternity series. It is a collection of short stories.

In the Mirror of Eternity – This is the first #mirrorofeternity story. It is dangerous to meddle in the past and perhaps even to observe it.

Jack London's Suicide Note – a fictitious exploration of the controversy surrounding Jack London's untimely death at the age of 40.

The Library – an encounter between two very different characters in cyberspace. These days libraries have computers and you can meet all sorts of people online.

Der Der, Der Der – the first Virginia Monologue story. Be warned, she might be quite amusing on the page but give her a wide berth in real life!

Guilt App – A story about the life of the rich and the chasm which exists between them and the 'people of the abyss.'

Paradox – Another adventure in cyberspace. The original story even had screenshots from a Commodore 64 but these have been sacrificed as the C64 now seems even more dated than I am.

Here be dragons – a story which explores the possibilities of travel in time and space. The 'dragon' in question may come as a surprise.

After Spartacus – Spartacus could be regarded as the first socialist – he thought the liberation of the oppressed was a job they could not leave to someone else. The Cross did become a symbol of Rome, but not in the way the Romans of the time imagined it would.

The SS Dagger – using the Mirror of Eternity to solve a murder in Nazi Germany produces an unexpected ending.

League of St George – a harmless drinking club celebrating the myth of St George hides something far more sinister.

The Stalker - I read the tabloid headlines most mornings. If the economy is going down the pan, they will have a headline about Big Brother. If the prime minister is at the centre of a scandal, EastEnders will be the big issue of the day. And I wonder exactly what the truth is behind their celebrity stories.

Virginia Monologue – the second Victoria Monologue story sees her talking to a friend who does not seem to be responding.

Doctor, it's about your car - The best way to get through to someone who is too busy to talk to you is to tell the switchboard "It's about his car." You will get through – even if they are "on a trip abroad" or "in a vital meeting" :)

Dramatoes - Childish pronunciation is always endearing. This story grew out of the way my son pronounced "dominoes".

Omar - This story is based on a personal experience when my wife and I were in Tunisia. I can tell you in advance that the ending was somewhat different in our case but that is all I will tell you before you read it.

The Inspector called - A story about a school inspector. You will have guessed by now that I was a teacher once upon a time and they drove me up the wall. Bear with me.

Schadenfreude - The borderland between waking and sleeping is a strange and sometimes frightening place. It is just as well it is 'all in the mind' isn't it?

The Hitch-hiker - "Don't take lifts from strangers" is all very well. But don't forget the hitch-hiker is a stranger too.

Stations of the Cross - I never "really" believed my father was dead. It was only later, much later, that I realised he wasn't dead. Not as long as he was remembered.

The Tower of the Moon - A romantic tryst with a twist.

When I think about you - This story has been rejected by magazines as "too shocking". So either read it and prepare to be shocked or give it a miss!

Salt Wars

Salt Wars is a myth of the foundation of the city-state of Salzburg. Salt Wars is a science fiction book. It contains mild sex and violence. It also contains some humour.

Xavier Hollands is an eccentric technologist. That sounds so much better than "mad scientist". Using his father's theoretical work he has found a way to create a hard astral projection. After testing this out with his girlfriend, Tilly, he is dragged into the Salt Wars by Wolf-Dietrich von Raitenau who wants to secure the future of Salzburg and his own future as its Prince-Archbishop.

They travel back in time to the town which will eventually become Salzburg. Xavier's astral projection is so strong that he comes into conflict with the "best man" of the town whom he defeats at the May Fair. He also develops a relationship with Krystyna, the daughter of his employer in the town and betrothed of the erstwhile best man.

Using Xavier's methods, Tilly intervenes to save Xavier and to thwart Wolf-Dietrich. Magus – a medieval Satanist – tries to use Krystyna to seduce Xavier and thus tie him to the town forever. When this plot fails because of Tilly's intervention there is a battle through time and space.

Wolf-Dietrich is hunted down like a literal wolf. Xavier meets his claustrophobic nightmare on a submarine which is then depth-charged and flooded with water. Tilly meets her fate in a school where she cannot control her class or stop them bullying a young boy called Gabriel. When Tilly realises that Gabriel is trying to push her towards suicide, he is unmasked as Magus.

The trio return to the town to fight the first salt war. Wolf-Dietrich brings about a successful conclusion by playing on the superstitious fears of the attackers.

The book also has diary entries from the characters which give an insight into their thinking.

The book ends with a teaser for the next Xavier Holland's story "The Archbishop's Torturer"..

The Miranda Revolution

Can a mother's love help bring down a vicious dictatorship? The dictator is a strong man but Miranda is a strong woman.

In this book, three characters, Wolf-Dietrich, Tilly and Xavier become involved with the battle to overthrow the Dictatorship. It is an adventure story in which the three of them fight evil in their own very different ways.

The Dictatorship described is generic and could apply to a number of countries. The gangsters control the streets and the Dictatorship controls the gangsters. The Dictator's consort, Miranda, is drawn into the revolution by realising one of the street-girls is her daughter. A religious movement which has been a safety valve of value to the Dictator is transformed by Miranda's visions through the 'mirror of eternity'

The Miranda Revolution is a book of light and shade. Although there is humour, there is also a serious side to it. Shelly encouraged the poor to seek a better world with the phrase, "Ye are many, they are few." The poor know only too well that the rich have the guns and tanks on their side. The book is a work of fiction but it suggests one way those problems could be overcome. It is a message of hope.

The Miranda Revolution is suitable for young adults. It contains sex and violence but none of it is graphic. Most of the sexual references illustrate the plight of the street-girls in the Dictatorship.

Mirror of Eternity Four

The fourth book in the #mirrorofeternity series explores such varied scenes as the realm of Arthurian legend and the dark hidden world of Satanism in the UK.

 "Joseph of Aramathea brought Christianity to these islands. He did not bring it in a bloody cup!" (Sir Gareth).

A little blunt but to the point. The Mirror of Eternity 4 gives a new take (Xavier's take) on what the sangreal was all about. It may surprise you. It will give Dan Brown a fit!

So if you have ever wondered what the sangreal (or holy grail) really represented; if you have wondered what kind of horses the four riders of the apocalypse rode or whether there really was a top and bottom of the round table, #mirrorofeternity4 will answer your questions. From a certain point of view.

This book will make you want to know more about the knights of the soi-disant 'round table' and about the Mirror of Eternity. It might make you want to avoid Satanism and Satanists like the plague. It will certainly intrigue you.

Space Dog Alfred

Space Dog Alfred is not part of the #mirrorofeternity series and it is aimed at a younger audience. It is the book which has had most success in the difficult business of getting libraries ,which have no money to spare, to buy copies.

The book tells the story of a French Bulldog who ends up going into space with Finbar Cool, a very dodgy street trader and uncle to Tom and Seren, the twins who accompany him. Finn brings his daughter, Abby, along too. Tom is delighted about Abby tagging along, Seren not so much.

On the planet they go to there is a group mind which is shared by Gai - sentient tree-like creatures - the Veck who are humans but have mastered unpowered flight and the people of Ardin who are small but perfectly formed. They worship death.

The group mind is not shared by creatures known as the Gnarl who are warlike and largely live underground.

It is an adventure story in which the powers of all the characters are tested to the maximum. Abby, captured by the slovenly Veck, realises that her selfishness is holding her back. Seren eventually comes to realise that Abby can change for the better. Tom finds out that he really doesn't know everything. Finn realises the futility of war. Alfred's bravery and his powers of perception make him into a hero. Like all French Bulldogs, he has the power to understand what humans (and other creatures) are thinking.

In the end good triumphs over evil. The heroes succeed in averting a war which would have cost thousands of lives. In doing so they also introduce the gnarl to the joy of storytelling. They prove that it is possible to win a battle by surrendering.

Domain of Dreams

In this book, I have returned to the short story format. I have had some success in selling short stories in the United States to Everyday Fiction and to Page and Spine and in Canada to Saturday Night Reader. I even had one published in the Worthing Herald! It has something for everyone – adventure, romance, mystery and humour. I put into my stories the things I like to read myself. I expect all writers do that :)

The Mirror of Eternity is a computer simulation which enables the user to look backwards (and occasionally forwards) in time. It deals with the paradox of time travel. Although science categorically tells you that you cannot travel in time, in your dreams and reveries you can go to any place and any time. I think that Domain of Dreams takes full advantage of the possibilities of the Mirror of Eternity. Opinions differ as to whether it provides access to a parallel universe or its effects are simply an illusion.

The main characters are Wolf-Dietrich von Raitenau, the Prince-Archbishop of Salzburg. Xavier Hollands, the eccentric technologist (he prefers that term to 'mad scientist'), his wife Tilly who shares the programming of the Mirror of Eternity and the narrator who has remained a shadowy figure in the previous four books.

I love the scope and freedom which Science Fiction and Fantasy brings. I also like the discipline of the short story. As Mark Twain said in apologising for writing a long letter to a friend, "I didn't have the time to write a short one."

I started writing when I was ten but I have been able to devote the time to it since I retired 50 years later. I have learnt a lot in the last five years both about writing and about the market for books. I have had some success in selling my self-published books to libraries and bookshops but it has been an interesting challenge.

My greatest joy is sharing my ideas with my wife, Angela, who is also my editor.

Note – I intended to call the book "Dreamscape" but there are a surprising number of books with that title.